Promises from God:

Jeremiah 29:11
"For I know the plans I have for you," says the Lord. "My plans are for good and not to harm you, my plans give you a hope and a future."

John 14:27
"I am leaving you with a gift- peace of mind and heart. And the peace I give is a gift the world cannot give. So don't be troubled or afraid."

Hebrews 13:5
The Lord will never leave you or forsake you.

Matthew 11:28
"Come to me, all you who are weary and troubled, and I will give you rest."

2 Thessalonians 3:1
God is faithful. He will strengthen and protect you.

There once was a happy, blonde little girl,
Who loved to sing, to dance, and to twirl.

Things weren't the same as they used to be,
For Brittany, everything had changed in her family.

Her little sister had died a few weeks before,
She had said her goodbyes, but still wanted more.

She pondered these thoughts as she began praying.
"Please let me know, God," was what she was saying.

Brittany had doubts clouding up her sweet mind.
"God, is my sister with You? Please send a sign."

The next day, Brittany wrote a sweet little note,
And tied it to a balloon so that it would float.

A letter sent to heaven to say, "I miss you!"
To know if things about Heaven are really true.

Before sending the message to her sister, Caroline-
She added, "Tell me about Heaven & please send a sign."

As she released the balloon up into the sky,
Brittany cried out in glee as she watched it fly!

Her heart felt free for she had let her thoughts out.
Then waited for a sign to help relieve her doubt.

A few days later a package came in the mail.
God had shown that His great love would not fail.

The package had a note to help erase all her fears,
But it was the book that
brought her family to tears.

For she had asked for a sign not knowing what it could be
The book <u>What About Heaven</u>- "It was special to me!"

It had become a favorite and she knew it by heart,
It was the last book her mom read as her sister did depart.

The book tells about Heaven and the love of God's Son,
Of a beautiful place with constant celebration!

It says in Heaven, everyone's bodies are healthy and new;
There are no troubles and no reason to ever feel blue.

Heaven's got no sickness, or sadness-that's so great!
That means my sister is dancing at Heaven's pearly gate!

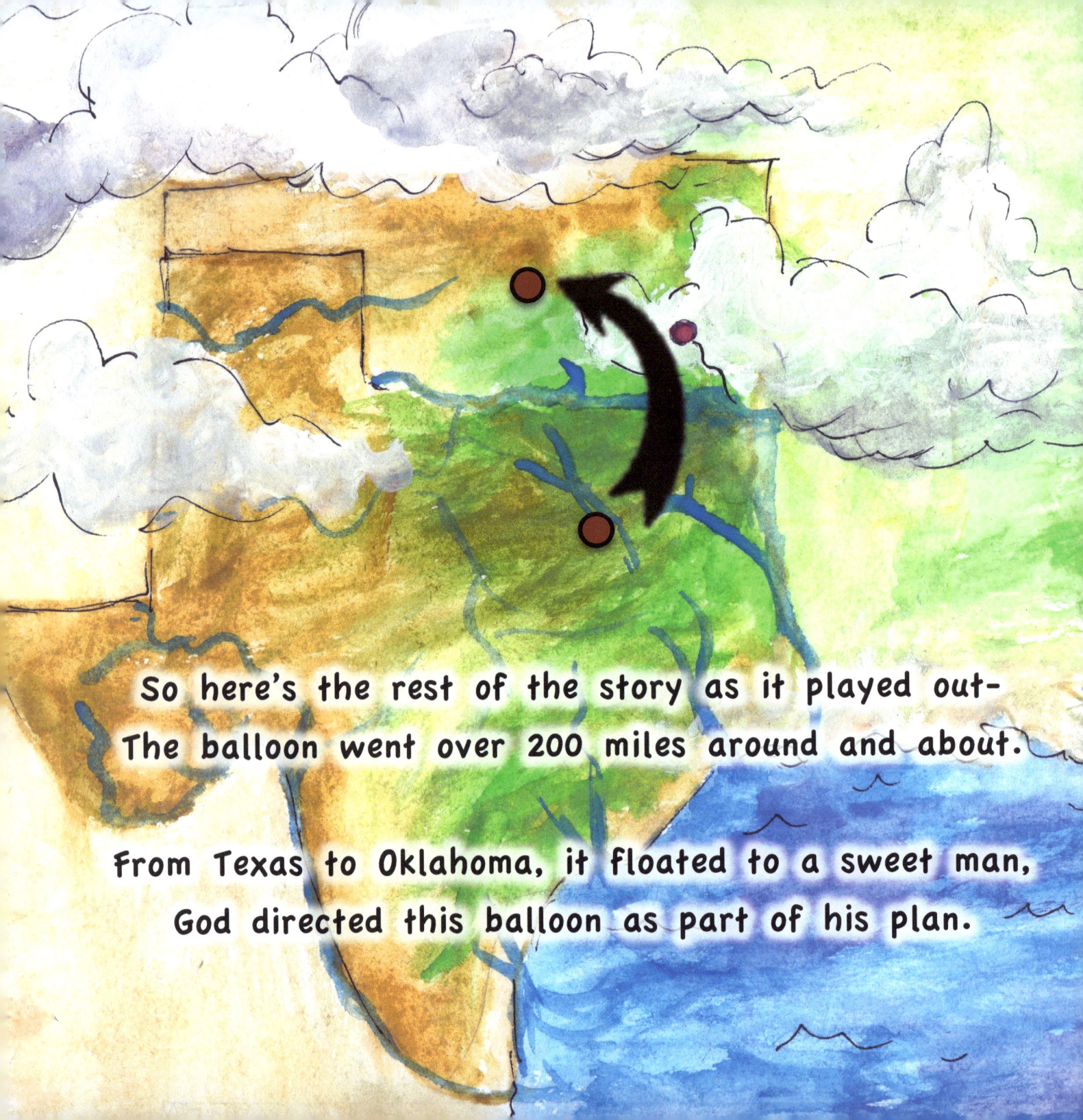

So here's the rest of the story as it played out-
The balloon went over 200 miles around and about.

From Texas to Oklahoma, it floated to a sweet man,
God directed this balloon as part of his plan.

After finding the note, the man prayed for what to do,
Not knowing his reply would be perfect and true.

The book was the sign- out of all the books in print,
<u>What About Heaven</u> is the one that the nice man sent.

It helped to show of our big God's great love,
He worked out this situation from up above.

God truly knows every little child's heart,
It shows He cares for our troubles-every part.

Brittany soon learned how to
stop the doubting thoughts-
She had found HOPE and it was helping lots!

The steps to defeat the doubt
were right in each letter—
H-O-P-E was how Brittany felt better.

"H" stands for <u>H</u>old on to the
Promises the Lord has made,
It is the first step in having
your doubts start to fade.

"O" is to <u>O</u>pen your eyes to see
God working in your life,
He's working things out for
your good from the strife.

"P" reminds us to talk
  to Him in our Prayers,
    For that's how to find out
      how much He cares.

"E" stands for Every doubt
  can be turned to the Lord;
    The Bible gives strength to slash
      doubts like a sword.

With HOPE Brittany found
    that God is in control;
        For every person, He has
            Plans that are wonderful!

Brittany exclaimed, "I
    know Heaven is for real!
        My Doubts are Defeated
            and my heart can now heal!"

The doubts were erased
    as this all came to be,
        For God orchestrated a
            miracle for all to see.

More Promises from God

Deuteronomy 31:6
Be strong and courageous. Do not fear or be anxious, for it is the LORD your God who goes with you. He will not leave you or forsake you.

Isaiah 41:10
"Do not fear, for I am with you; be not troubled, for I am your God; I will strengthen you, I will help you, I will uphold you with my righteous right hand."

Romans 8:39
Neither height nor depth, nor anything else in all creation, will be able to separate us from the love of God that is in Christ Jesus our Lord.

Philippians 4:19
God will supply all your needs from his glorious riches, which have been given to us in Christ Jesus.

Psalm 37:4
Delight yourself in the Lord, and he will give you the desires of your heart.

The Letter to Heaven and the Miraculous Reply

In 1999, I had become a big sister again. My other sister, Victoria, and I welcomed home my littlest sister, Caroline. We were three baby girls born in three years, and I was so excited to have someone else to play with! But after a few months, my parents were taking Caroline to appointments with doctors, CT scans, MRIs, and eventually, we received terrible news. The neurologist told us that Caroline's brain was dying. Caroline had been diagnosed with a rare degenerative brain disease that caused parts of her brain to shrink and other parts to calcify. There was no known cause and certainly no cure, and we were told that Baby Caroline would not likely live to see her first birthday. But on February 5, 2000, with all our extended family around, we lit a single candle on top of a cake, as Victoria and I led our family in "Happy Birthday." My parents knew that Caroline's time on earth would be short, so they vowed to make her life special, by making the best of everyday, as each passing day could have been her last. We took pictures almost daily to document her precious life. The three of us played beauty shop with make-up and fixed hair, played in dress up clothes, splashed in the pool, and played make-believe. On February 5, 2001, we again celebrated as Caroline turned 2, despite the fact that she was unable to move any part of her little body and had continual seizures. On July 8, 2001, my mom read the book <u>What About Heaven</u> by Kathy Bostrom to Victoria and I, as little Caroline was in her arms. We had read it many times, as it was comforting to hear about how wonderful Heaven is as the book says "your body will change so it's perfect and new, and yet you will be the very same you." "Sadness and pain will be taken away. Once you are there, you will be happy to stay." Caroline went to be with the Lord just a few hours later that day.

Six weeks after Caroline died, I came home from kindergarten wanting to tell my little sister in Heaven a message. My mom suggested that I write what I wanted to say to her, then we decided to send the message to her tied to a balloon. My letter said:

Dear Caroline,
Hi, sweet baby sister! We want to write to you since you passed away and tell you how much we love you! We want to hold you again, and cannot wait to see you in Heaven someday. We will never forget you or your smile or your laugh.   All our love, Brittany & Victoria

Almost ready to walk outside to release the balloon, I then asked my mom to also write on the note: *P.S. We want to get a sign from you that you are with Jesus and that you know we love you.* I remember hugging that brightly colored mylar balloon before releasing it to fly to Heaven.

The gusty wing on that September day quickly carried the balloon away. We stood in front of our house and stared into the sky until we could no longer see it. As we went to bed that evening, a big storm blew through our little Dallas suburb of Southlake, and we wondered if the balloon would even survive the night.

Days after the balloon rose into the clouds, past lakes, rivers, pastures, and small towns, it landed on a cattle ranch in El Reno, Oklahoma, where David Griesel saw something shiny while looking after his herd. He found the balloon with its ribbon tangled in a cedar tree, and the letter stopped him cold. David, along with a co-worker, Milea Gundlach wrote a note back, and placed their sweet letter along with a copy of the book, <u>What About Heaven</u>. Immediately upon seeing the book, I burst out, "It's the sign that Caroline is with Jesus!"

This so vividly and clearly showed how much God cares for me. I really believe God orchestrated these events in such a way to help my five-year-old heart not hurt so much and to share the miracle so that others could see His great love! The story was printed in the *Fort Worth Star Telegram* newspaper in an article entitled, "Destination: Heaven" on Sunday, December 16, 2001, and was placed on the AP wire for newspapers around the country and world. Again, it was told on May 21, 2002 in *Woman's World Magazine* in the article, "Letter to Heaven."

www.ingramcontent.com/pod-product-compliance
Lightning Source LLC
Chambersburg PA
CBHW041230040426

42444CB00002B/110